MW01232126

CLASSICAL TURKISH COOKING

SIMPLE, EASY, AND UNIQUE TURKISH RECIPES

By
Umm Maryam
Copyright © 2015 by Saxonberg
Associates

Published by
BookSumo, a division of Saxonberg
Associates
http://www.booksumo.com/

A GIFT FROM ME TO YOU...

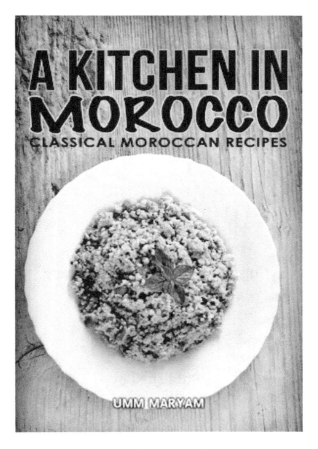

Send the Book!

Hey thanks for purchasing my cookbook. If you join my private reader's club you will get one of my favorite books: *A Kitchen in Morocco: Classical Moroccan Recipes.*

This cookbook has over 35 amazing Moroccan and West African recipes that you will absolutely LOVE! It is not available to anyone else, except private readers.

You'll learn how to make classical Moroccan Cous Cous, Peanut Stews, Tagine, Cous Cous Kebabs and a lot more. So join my club!

You will also receive updates about all my new books when they are free. So please show your support.

Also don't forget to like and subscribe on the social networks. I love meeting my readers. Links to all my profiles are below so please click and connect :)

Facebook

Twitter

Google +

About the Author.

Umm Maryam is a self-proclaimed lover of culture. She focuses her time on writing books about different countries in the Arab and Asian world.

CLASSICAL TURKISH
COOKING
SIMPLE, EASY, AND UNIQUE TURKISH RECIPES

UMM MARYAM

UMM MARYAM

CLASSICAL LEBANESE
COOKING
SIMPLE, EASY, AND UNIQUE LEBANESE RECIPES

UMM MARYAM

ARABIA & ASIA
A COOKBOOK WITH RECIPES FROM
EGYPT, MOROCCO, PERSIA, & PAKISTAN

UMM MARYAM

CLASSICAL INDIAN
COOKING
SIMPLE, EASY, AND UNIQUE INDIAN RECIPES

For a complete listing of all my books please see my author page at:

http://amazon.com/author/ummmaryam

INTRODUCTION

Hello, my friend. I would like to thank you personally for taking the time to purchase my book: *Classical Turkish Cooking: Simple, Easy, and Unique Turkish Recipes.* I truly do hope that these recipes are reaching you in the best of health and a period of happiness.

In writing this book I have taken the time to compile, what I believe to be, the simplest and easiest, classical Turkish dishes into one source for those of my readers who are cultural food lovers.

After publishing my first book: *Arabia & Asia: A Cookbook with Recipes from Egypt, Morocco, Persia, & Pakistan* I noticed a strong interest in this type of food. So I made the decision to continue this cooking journey by focusing on a new country.

If you are interested in my first cookbook then please see the last few pages of this book where I've provided a link for where to find my seminal cookbook.

If you are interested in any specific type of food then please let me know. I'm very easy to find :)

In writing this book, I have tried to improve the style and content since my last cookbook. For each recipe, you will read in *Classical Turkish Cooking: Simple, Easy, and Unique Turkish Recipes* I've taken the care to provide not only ingredients with specific directions. But I've also tried to provide accurate information on the amount of time it will take to prepare and cook each dish, so you can plan accordingly before embarking on a specific cooking journey. Each recipe also contains information on its nutritional value as well as serving information. So for my health conscience readers check the caloric and fat contents of each dish.

I really want to provide the most value for you, my readers, so I figured this information will help a bit more. I'm constantly trying to improve and I listen to my readers. So please help me with feedback!

You'll find that many of the recipes require a lot of spice so make sure you have a lot of the following ingredients: coriander, cumin, yogurt, salt, pepper, cayenne, fresh garlic and onions, turmeric, and curry.

So without further ado, I will stop talking. Let's get our frying pans and food processors ready and take a trip to Turkey with some simple and easy recipes!

TABLE OF CONTENTS

NOTICE TO PRINT READERS:

Hey, because you purchased the print version of this book you are entitled to its original digital version for free by Amazon.

So when you have the time, please review your purchases, and download the Kindle version of this book.

You might enjoy consuming this book more in its original digital format.

;)

But, in any case, take care and enjoy reading in whatever format you choose!

LEGAL NOTES

Chapter 1: Simple, Easy, and Unique Turkish Recipes

Turkish Fish Stew

Ingredients

- 3 cups water
- 1 1/2 cups dry couscous
- 2 tbsps olive oil
- 1 small white onion, chopped
- 1 green bell pepper, chopped
- 2 cloves garlic, minced
- 1 cup marinated artichoke hearts, liquid reserved
- 2 tsps capers, liquid reserved
- 12 small green olives
- 1 (14.5 ounce) can chopped stewed tomatoes, drained
- 2 tbsps white wine(optional)
- 1 tbsp lemon juice
- 1 cup water
- 2 tsps sumac powder

- 1 1/2 tsps crushed red pepper flakes
- 1 tsp dried basil
- 1 tsp cumin
- 1 tsp minced fresh ginger root
- ground black pepper to taste
- 1 pound tilapia fillets, cut into chunks

☐

Directions

- Add couscous into boiling water before turning the heat off and letting it stand as it is for about 5 minutes.
- Cook onion and green pepper in hot olive oil for about five minutes before adding garlic and cooking it for another two minutes.
- Stir in artichoke hearts, capers and some olives before adding tomatoes, water, wine, red pepper, ginger, pepper, cumin, sumac powder, basil and lemon juice before bringing this all to boil.
- Stir in fish chunks before turning the heat down and cooking all this for another ten minutes.

- Serve this over couscous in a platter.

Serving: 4

Timing Information:

Preparation	Cooking	Total Time
15 mins	30 mins	45 mins

Nutritional Information:

Calories	456 kcal
Carbohydrates	53.4 g
Cholesterol	42 mg
Fat	12.4 g
Fiber	6.3 g
Protein	32.7 g
Sodium	755 mg

* Percent Daily Values are based on a 2,000 calorie diet.

Haydari

(A Turkish Yogurt Dip)

Ingredients

- 1 (16 ounce) container plain yogurt
- 5 cloves garlic
- 1 pinch salt
- 1 bunch fresh dill, chopped
- 1 bunch fresh parsley, chopped
- 1 (4 ounce) package cream cheese, softened (optional)
- 2 mint leaves, for garnish

Directions

- Place a colander having cheesecloth over a medium sized bowl and put yoghurt on the cheesecloth before covering the colander with plastic wrap and letting it stand as it is for 8 hours.
- Add mashed salt and garlic in a bowl containing drained yoghurt

before adding cream cheese, dill
and parsley into it.

- Place it on serving dish and
garnish with mint leaves before
serving.

Serving: 8

Timing Information:

Preparation	Cooking	Total Time
15 mins		8 hr 15 mins

Nutritional Information:

Calories	92 kcal
Carbohydrates	5.7 g
Cholesterol	19 mg
Fat	5.9 g
Fiber	0.4 g
Protein	4.5 g
Sodium	88 mg

* Percent Daily Values are based on a 2,000 calorie diet.

TAVA I

(A TURKISH STEW)

Ingredients

- 2 tbsps olive oil, divided
- 1 1/2 pounds skinless, boneless chicken breast halves - cut into 1 inch cubes
- 1/2 (12 ounce) jar roasted red bell peppers, drained
- 1 (14.5 ounce) can diced tomatoes with juice
- 1 (6 ounce) jar mushrooms, drained
- 1 onion, diced
- 1 tbsp minced garlic
- salt and pepper to taste
- 1 (16 ounce) package shredded mozzarella cheese

Directions

- Preheat your oven to 350 degrees F and put some oil on the casserole dish.

- Cook chicken in hot oil for a few minutes.
- Blend roasted red peppers in a blender before mixing these peppers, cooked chicken, garlic, mushrooms, tomatoes and onion in the prepared casserole dish.
- Add salt, pepper, olive oil and on top of all this, put mozzarella cheese.
- Bake in the preheated oven for about 30 minutes or until the cheese is melted.
- Serve.

Serving: 6

Timing Information:

Preparation	Cooking	Total Time
15 mins	40 mins	55 mins

Nutritional Information:

Calories	397 kcal
Carbohydrates	9.4 g
Cholesterol	113 mg
Fat	19.5 g
Fiber	1.8 g
Protein	43.7 g
Sodium	854 mg

* Percent Daily Values are based on a 2,000 calorie diet. □

DONDURMA

(TURKISH ICE CREAM)

Ingredients

- 1 1/2 cups water
- 2 cups white sugar
- 1 1/2 cups heavy cream
- 1 1/2 cups milk
- 6 egg yolks
- 3 tbsps instant coffee granules
- 2 tbsps finely ground coffee (optional)

Directions

- Bring a mixture of water and sugar to boil until you see that the sugar has completely before adding this, cream and milk into a double boiler.
- When completely mixed; add egg yolks and instant coffee.
- Set the boiler over a pan containing hot water before

cooking it for another ten
minutes.

- Pour this into a bowl using mesh
  strainer and add coffee grounds
  before refrigerating it for one full
  hour.
- Pour this mixture into an ice
  cream maker and freeze it
  according to the directions of
  manufacturer.

Serving: 8

Timing Information:

Preparation	Cooking	Total Time
10 mins	20 mins	7 hr 30 mins

Nutritional Information:

Calories	413 kcal
Carbohydrates	54.4 g
Cholesterol	218 mg
Fat	20.7 g
Fiber	0 g
Protein	4.6 g
Sodium	44 mg

* Percent Daily Values are based on a 2,000 calorie diet.

☐

Breakfast Eggs in Turkey

Ingredients

- 3 cloves garlic, peeled and minced
- 1 1/2 cups plain yogurt
- 1 pinch salt
- 1 quart water
- 1 tbsp vinegar
- 1 tsp salt
- 6 eggs
- 2 tbsps butter
- 1 tsp paprika

Directions

- Mix garlic, salt and yoghurt in a small bowl.
- Bring the mixture of water, salt and vinegar to boil over high heat before turning the heat down and adding eggs into the pan.
- When the eggs are set; Transfer them to a serving platter.

- Put yoghurt over these eggs and on top of all this, add mixture of melted butter and some paprika.
- Serve.

Serving: 2

Timing Information:

Preparation	Cooking	Total Time
15 mins	5 mins	20 mins

Nutritional Information:

Calories	442 kcal
Carbohydrates	16.2 g
Cholesterol	600 mg
Fat	29.4 g
Fiber	0.5 g
Protein	29.1 g
Sodium	1599 mg

* Percent Daily Values are based on a 2,000 calorie diet.

A Turkish Soup of Red Lentils

Ingredients

- 1/4 cup butter
- 2 onions, finely chopped
- 1 tsp paprika
- 1 cup red lentils
- 1/2 cup fine bulgur
- 2 tbsps tomato paste
- 8 cups vegetable stock
- 1/8 tsp cayenne pepper
- 1 tbsp dried mint leaves
- 4 slices lemon
- 1/2 tsp chopped fresh mint

Directions

- Cook onion in hot butter for about 15 minutes before adding paprika, bulgur and lentil into it.
- Bring the mixture to boil after adding cayenne pepper, tomato sauce and vegetable stock into the

pan, and cook all this for one full hour.

- Stir in some mint leaves before turning the heat off and pouring the soup in reasonable bowls.
- Garnish with some lemon slices and fresh mint before serving.

Serving: 6

Timing Information:

Preparation	Cooking	Total Time
10 mins	1 hr 15 mins	1 hr 25 mins

Nutritional Information:

Calories	442 kcal
Carbohydrates	64.2 g
Cholesterol	31 mg
Fat	14 g
Fiber	15.1 g
Protein	18.7 g
Sodium	1080 mg

* Percent Daily Values are based on a 2,000 calorie diet.

CLASSICAL TURKISH GREENS

Ingredients

- 2 cups beet greens
- 7 dried Turkish figs, stemmed and quartered
- 1/2 cup Riesling wine
- 2 cups fresh spinach
- 1 clove garlic, minced
- 2 tsps butter
- salt to taste
- 1/2 ounce grated Parmesan cheese (optional)

Directions

- Cook beet greens, Riesling wine and figs over medium in a pan for about seven minutes before adding butter, spinach and garlic.
- Turn the heat down to low and cook for another three minutes before adding some salt.
- Put some parmesan cheese on top of all these vegetables before serving.

Serving: 2

Timing Information:

Preparation	Cooking	Total Time
10 mins	10 mins	20 mins

Nutritional Information:

Calories	328 kcal
Carbohydrates	49.4 g
Cholesterol	17 mg
Fat	7 g
Fiber	10.2 g
Protein	6.7 g
Sodium	260 mg

* Percent Daily Values are based on a 2,000 calorie diet.□

MANTI

(TURKISH RAVIOLI)

Ingredients

- 1 tsp salt
- 1 tsp dried mint
- 1 (9 ounce) package beef ravioli
- 1/4 cup butter
- 1 tsp sweet paprika
- 1 tbsp minced garlic
- 1 (8 ounce) container plain whole milk yogurt

Directions

- Cook salt, ravioli and mint in boiling water for five minutes before draining it.
- Melt butter over a pan and add paprika before setting it aside to cool down.
- Put yoghurt and garlic mixture over ravioli before adding that melted on top of all this.
- Serve.

Serving: 4

Timing Information:

Preparation	Cooking	Total Time
10 mins	10 mins	20 mins

Nutritional Information:

Calories	293 kcal
Carbohydrates	26.7 g
Cholesterol	60 mg
Fat	17.1 g
Fiber	2.5 g
Protein	9.4 g
Sodium	1098 mg

* Percent Daily Values are based on a 2,000 calorie diet.

TURKISH COOKIES

Ingredients

- 2 cups all-purpose flour
- 1 cup butter, softened
- 1 cup confectioners' sugar
- 1 egg
- 1 tsp vanilla extract
- 1/4 cup strawberry preserves

Directions

- Combine flour, butter or margarine, confectioners' sugar, egg and vanilla in a bowl very thoroughly before making 1.5 inch round doughs from it.
- Place these on the baking sheet before making some place in the dough and placing jam.
- Bake this at 350 degrees F for about twelve minutes or until you see that the bottoms are lightly brown.

Serving: 18

Timing Information:

Preparation	Cooking	Total Time
10 mins	10 mins	20 mins

Nutritional Information:

Calories	551 kcal
Carbohydrates	61 g
Cholesterol	112 mg
Fat	32 g
Fiber	1.3 g
Protein	5.7 g
Sodium	235 mg

* Percent Daily Values are based on a 2,000 calorie diet.

A TURKISH INSPIRED CEVICHE

Ingredients

- 1 lemon, halved and seeded
- 1 head garlic, halved
- 3 Turkish bay leaves
- 8 whole black peppercorns
- 1 tbsp kosher salt, or to taste
- 1 1/2 pounds peeled and deveined large shrimp (21 to 25 per lb)
- 2 cups coconut milk
- 1/2 cup lime juice
- 2 serrano chile peppers, thinly sliced
- 1/2 bunch cilantro, chopped
- 1 red onion, thinly sliced
- 8 sprigs cilantro, for garnish
- 1 lime, cut into 8 wedges

Directions

- Bring a mixture of garlic, salt, squeezed lemon and its juice, bay leaves, water and peppercorns to boil over high heat before adding shrimp and turning the heat off.

- Let it stand as it is for five minutes.
- Drain this using a colander before letting it cool down for thirty minutes in baking dish.
- Add shrimp that is cut in half lengthwise into the mixture of coconut milk, serrano peppers, chopped cilantro, lime juice and onion before refrigerating it for 30 minutes.
- Garnish with lime wedges and cilantro sprigs before serving.

Serving: 8

Timing Information:

Preparation	Cooking	Total Time
15 mins	5 mins	1 hr 20 mins

Nutritional Information:

Calories	207 kcal
Carbohydrates	9.9 g
Cholesterol	129 mg
Fat	13 g
Fiber	2.5 g
Protein	16.2 g
Sodium	882 mg

* Percent Daily Values are based on a 2,000 calorie diet.

KISIR

(A TURKISH BULGUR AND VEGETABLE SALAD)

Ingredients

- 1 cup fine bulgur
- 1 cup boiling water
- 2 tbsps olive oil
- 1 onion, finely chopped
- 2 large tomatoes, finely chopped
- 1 cucumber, diced
- 2 green bell peppers, finely chopped
- 1 red bell peppers, finely chopped
- 7 green onions, finely chopped
- 1/2 cup minced fresh parsley
- 1/2 cup minced fresh mint leaves
- 1 tsp red pepper flakes, or to taste
- 2 tbsps olive oil
- juice of 1 fresh lemon
- 2 tbsps pomegranate molasses

Directions

- Let the bulgur stand in boiling water for twenty minutes.

- In that time, cook onion in hot oil for about five minutes.
- Mix bulgur, mint, cooked onion, cucumber, green and red bell peppers, chopped tomatoes, green onions, olive oil, pomegranate molasses, parsley, lemon juice and red pepper flakes in a bowl very thoroughly before serving.

Serving: 6

Timing Information:

Preparation	Cooking	Total Time
15 mins	5 mins	40 mins

Nutritional Information:

Calories	216 kcal
Carbohydrates	30.4 g
Cholesterol	0 mg
Fat	9.8 g
Fiber	7.7 g
Protein	5.3 g
Sodium	19 mg

* Percent Daily Values are based on a 2,000 calorie diet.

CLASSICAL BULGUR

Ingredients

- 3 tbsps olive oil
- 1 onion, minced
- 1 ripe tomato, cut into small cubes
- 3 cups beef broth
- 2 cups bulgur, rinsed
- salt and ground black pepper, or to taste
- 1/2 cup cooked green lentils
- 1/3 cup cooked chickpeas
- 1 bunch fresh mint, chopped

Directions

- Cook onion in hot oil for about three minutes before adding tomatoes and cooking it for another two minutes.
- Add beef broth into this pan before bring all this to boil.
- Now put bulgur, black pepper and salt into the mixture, and cook all this for five minutes

before adding lentils and chickpeas, and cooking all this for another five minutes or until you see that the bulgur is tender.

- Let it cool down for 30 minutes before adding some mint for the purpose of serving.

Serving: 6

Timing Information:

Preparation	Cooking	Total Time
15 mins	15 mins	1 hr

Nutritional Information:

Calories	323 kcal
Carbohydrates	53.1 g
Cholesterol	0 mg
Fat	8.1 g
Fiber	14.9 g
Protein	12.8 g
Sodium	511 mg

* Percent Daily Values are based on a 2,000 calorie diet.

☐

TAVA II

(TURKISH STEW)

Ingredients

- 2 tbsps olive oil, divided
- 8 boneless chicken thighs, with skin
- 1 (6 ounce) can tomato paste
- 1/4 cup water
- 8 cloves garlic, halved
- salt and pepper to taste
- 4 medium potatoes, sliced
- 4 tomatoes, sliced
- 1 large onion, sliced
- 1 cup fresh mushrooms, sliced
- 8 pepperoncini peppers(optional)

Directions

- Preheat your oven to 350 degrees F and put some oil over the quiche dish.
- On top of chicken thighs in a baking dish containing some olive oil; add tomato sauce, pepper,

potatoes, pepperoncini, tomatoes, mushrooms and onions before pouring the remaining olive oil over all this.

- Bake in the preheated oven for about 90 minutes or until you see that the vegetables are tender.

Serving: 8

Timing Information:

Preparation	Cooking	Total Time
20 mins	30 mins	1 hr 50 mins

Nutritional Information:

Calories	316 kcal
Carbohydrates	29 g
Cholesterol	59 mg
Fat	13.7 g
Fiber	4.7 g
Protein	20.4 g
Sodium	823 mg

* Percent Daily Values are based on a 2,000 calorie diet.

☐

Iskender Kebabs

Ingredients

- 4 pita bread rounds
- 1 tbsp olive oil
- 4 skinless, boneless chicken breast halves - chopped
- 2 medium onion, chopped
- 1 clove garlic, minced
- 1 (10.75 ounce) can tomato puree
- ground cumin to taste
- salt to taste
- ground black pepper to taste
- 1/2 cup butter, melted
- 1 cup Greek yogurt
- 1/4 cup chopped fresh parsley

Directions

- Preheat your oven to 350 degrees F and bake pita bread in it for some time before cutting it down into small pieces.
- Cook garlic, chicken and onion in hot oil for some time before adding tomato puree, pepper, salt

and cumin, and cooking it for another ten minutes.

- On top of pita bread in a serving platter; put chicken mixture and some butter.
- Garnish with some parsley and yoghurt before you serve it.

Serving: 4

Timing Information:

Preparation	Cooking	Total Time
15 mins	15 mins	30 mins

Nutritional Information:

Calories	667 kcal
Carbohydrates	48.6 g
Cholesterol	144 mg
Fat	36.2 g
Fiber	3.9 g
Protein	37.3 g
Sodium	886 mg

* Percent Daily Values are based on a 2,000 calorie diet.

☐

Moussaka

(Potato Casserole from the Ottoman Empire)

Ingredients

- 5 tbsps olive oil
- 1 pound ground beef
- 1 tsp ground paprika
- 1 tsp ground cumin
- 1 tsp salt
- 1 tsp ground black pepper
- 4 potatoes, peeled and cut into 1/2-inch cubes
- 1 (6.5 ounce) can tomato sauce
- 1 tbsp chopped summer savory (chubritsa)
- 1 egg, lightly beaten
- 2/3 cup yogurt

Directions

- Preheat your oven to 325 degrees F.
- Cook ground beef in hot oil until you see that it is brown from all sides before adding paprika,

pepper, cumin, tomatoes and salt into it, and cooking it for another three minutes.

- After turning the heat down to low and adding tomato sauce; cook all this for 15 more minutes.
- Now pour the mixture of egg and yoghurt over this meat mixture in the baking dish.
- Bake in the preheated oven for about 40 minutes or until the top is golden brown in color.

Serving: 5

Timing Information:

Preparation	Cooking	Total Time
15 mins	45 mins	1 hr

Nutritional Information:

Calories	728 kcal
Carbohydrates	44.3 g
Cholesterol	145 mg
Fat	49.4 g
Fiber	6.2 g
Protein	27.8 g
Sodium	961 mg

* Percent Daily Values are based on a 2,000 calorie diet.

Dukkah

(Levantine Spice Mix)

Ingredients

- 2/3 cup hazelnuts
- 1/2 cup sesame seeds
- 2 tbsps coriander seeds
- 2 tbsps cumin seeds
- 2 tbsps freshly ground black pepper
- 1 tsp flaked sea salt

Directions

- Remove the skin from hazelnuts by rubbing after baking in a preheated oven at 350 degrees for five minutes.
- Toast sesame seeds, coriander and cumin seeds separately in a pan until golden brown before placing them in the blender.
- Blend them one by one, so that the end product is smooth.

- Add hazelnuts in the blender and blend all the content until you see that everything is finely crushed.
- Transfer to a bowl and mix it well with spices, and season with salt and pepper according to your taste.
- Serve.

NOTE: Use this spice as topping for any type of toasted bread. Super addictive.

Serving: 2

Timing Information:

Preparation	Cooking	Total Time
20 mins	5 mins	25 mins

Nutritional Information:

Calories	45 kcal
Carbohydrates	2.1 g
Cholesterol	0 mg
Fat	4 g
Fiber	1.1 g
Protein	1.3 g
Sodium	75 mg

* Percent Daily Values are based on a 2,000 calorie diet.

Classical Turkish Chevre

Ingredients

- 1 (8 ounce) log of fresh goat cheese (chevre)
- 1/2 tsp Urfa biber, or to taste
- 2 tbsps finely crushed cocoa nibs

Directions

- Mix urfa biber and goat cheese (that has been placed at room temperature for about 30 minutes) in a bowl before wrapping it around a plastic to get it into log shape by placing it in the freezer for about one hour.
- Coat cocoa nibs very thorough with this cheese before wrapping it up again to be chilled for one more hour.
- Serve this after bringing this to room temperature.

Serving: 8

Timing Information:

Preparation	Cooking	Total Time
10 mins	2 hr 30 mins	2 hr 40 mins

Nutritional Information:

Calories	96 kcal
Carbohydrates	1.7 g
Cholesterol	18 mg
Fat	7.6 g
Fiber	0.7 g
Protein	5 g
Sodium	119 mg

* Percent Daily Values are based on a 2,000 calorie diet.

SHAKSHOUKA

(LEVANTINE SPICY EGGS)

Ingredients

- 3 tbsps olive oil
- 1 1/3 cups chopped onion
- 1 cup thinly sliced bell peppers, any color
- 2 cloves garlic, minced, or to taste
- 2 1/2 cups chopped tomatoes
- 1 tsp ground cumin
- 1 tsp paprika
- 1 tsp salt
- 1 hot chile pepper, seeded and finely chopped, or to taste
- 4 eggs

Directions

- Cook onion, garlic and bell peppers in hot oil for about five minutes or until you see that the vegetables have softened up.
- Add the mixture of chili pepper, tomatoes, salt, cumin and paprika

into this pan before cooking it for another ten minutes.

- Make space for eggs in the mixture and cook these eggs by covering the pan, and cooking it for five minutes or until the eggs are firm.
- Serve.

Serving: 4

Timing Information:

Preparation	Cooking	Total Time
20 mins	20 mins	40 mins

Nutritional Information:

Calories	209 kcal
Carbohydrates	12.9 g
Cholesterol	164 mg
Fat	15 g
Fiber	3.1 g
Protein	7.8 g
Sodium	654 mg

* Percent Daily Values are based on a 2,000 calorie diet.

DOLMAS

(STUFFED GRAPE LEAVES)

Ingredients

- 1 tbsp olive oil
- 2 onions, minced
- 1 1/2 cups uncooked white rice
- 2 tbsps tomato paste
- 2 tbsps dried currants
- 2 tbsps pine nuts
- 1 tbsp ground cinnamon
- 1 tbsp dried mint
- 1 tbsp dried dill weed
- 1 tsp ground allspice
- 1 tsp ground cumin
- 1 (8 ounce) jar grape leaves, drained and rinsed

Directions

- Cook onion in hot oil until tender before adding rice and hot water, and cooking all this for ten minutes or until the rice is cooked.

- Turn the heat off and stir in tomato paste, allspice, currants, mint leaves, pine nuts, cinnamon, dill weed, allspice and cumin.
- Place rinse grape leaves in warm water before cutting the stems and filling the center of leaf with cooked rice.
- Fold it up and place in the pot having inverted plate at the bottom.
- Add enough water to cover the dolmas and cook it over low heat for about 45 minutes.
- Serve.

Serving: 8

Timing Information:

Preparation	Cooking	Total Time
30 mins	45 mins	1 hr 15 mins

Nutritional Information:

Calories	207 kcal
Carbohydrates	39.1 g
Cholesterol	0 mg
Fat	3.8 g
Fiber	2 g
Protein	5.3 g
Sodium	847 mg

* Percent Daily Values are based on a 2,000 calorie diet.

A GIFT FROM ME TO YOU...

Send the Book!

Hey thanks for purchasing my cookbook. If you join my private reader's club you will get one of my favorite books: *A Kitchen in Morocco: Classical Moroccan Recipes.*

This cookbook has over 35 amazing Moroccan and West African recipes that you will absolutely LOVE! It is not available to anyone else, except private readers.

You'll learn how to make classical Moroccan Cous Cous, Peanut Stews, Tagine, Cous Cous Kebabs and a lot more. So join my club!

You will also receive updates about all my new books when they are free. So please show your support.

Also don't forget to like and subscribe on the social networks. I love meeting my readers. Links to all my profiles are below so please click and connect :)

Facebook

Twitter

Google +

COME ON...
LET'S BE FRIENDS :)

I adore my readers and love connecting with them socially. Please follow the links below so we can connect on Facebook, Twitter, and Google+.

Facebook

Twitter

Google +

I also have a blog that I regularly update for my readers so check it out below.

My Blog

Can I Ask A Favour?

If you found this book interesting, or have otherwise found any benefit in it. Then may I ask that you post a review of it on Amazon? Nothing excites me more than new reviews, especially reviews which suggest new topics for writing. I do read all reviews and I always factor feedback into my newer works.

So if you are willing to take ten minutes to write what you sincerely thought about this book then please visit our Amazon page and post your opinions.

Again thank you!

INTERESTED IN MY OTHER COOKBOOKS?

For more great cookbooks check out my Amazon Author page:

For a complete listing of all my books please see my author page at:

*http://amazon.com/author/ummmary
am*

Made in the USA
Columbia, SC
10 September 2023

22699322R10046